Desert Fathers,

Uranium Daughters

■ ■

Other books by the author

■ ■

MOVABLE ISLANDS

AND

THE 1002ND NIGHT

OFF-SEASON AT THE EDGE OF THE WORLD

Desert Fathers,

Uranium Daughters

———————

Debora Greger

PENGUIN POETS

PENGUIN BOOKS
Published by the Penguin Group
Penguin Books USA Inc., 375 Hudson Street,
New York, New York 10014, U.S.A.
Penguin Books Ltd, 27 Wrights Lane,
London W8 5TZ, England
Penguin Books Australia Ltd, Ringwood,
Victoria, Australia
Penguin Books Canada Ltd, 10 Alcorn Avenue,
Toronto, Ontario, Canada M4V 3B2
Penguin Books (N.Z.) Ltd, 182–190 Wairau Road,
Auckland 10, New Zealand

Penguin Books Ltd, Registered Offices:
Harmondsworth, Middlesex, England

First published in Penguin Books 1996

1 3 5 7 9 10 8 6 4 2

Page xiii constitutes an extension of this copyright page.

LIBRARY OF CONGRESS CATALOGING IN PUBLICATION DATA
Greger, Debora, 1949–
Desert fathers, uranium daughters/Debora Greger.
p.   cm.
ISBN 0 14 05.8774 8 (pbk)
I. Title.
PS3557.R42D47   1996
811'.54—dc20   96–6278

Printed in the United States of America
Set in Walbaum MT
Designed by Claire Vaccaro

For my father, Greg,
and my mother, Margaret,
and for Miriam, Joel, Jan,
Amelie, Del, and Evan

God help me from inventing when I sing.

—NERUDA

Acknowledgments

Field: "Keats in Ohio"

The Gettysburg Review: "The Flea Market at the End of History," "Memories of the Atomic Age"

The Nation: "Adam's Daughter," "The Age of Reason," "The Desert Father," "The Desert Fathers: The Flagpole-Sitter," "In the Eternal City," "The Love of Ruins," "Much Too Late," "Northwest Passage," "The Patron Saint of Venice," "Ship Burial: Hanford, Washington," "Sunday at the Ruins"

The New Republic: "The Further Travels of Marco Polo," "Nights of 1995"

The New Yorker: "I Dinosauri di Venezia"

Parnassus: "Andante Pastorale"

Poetry: "The Blessing of the Throats," "The Cloud of Unknowing," "In the Museum of the Eighteenth Century," "Lives of the North American Martyrs," "Psyche and Eros in Florida," "Sacre Conversazioni"

The Sewanee Review: "Il Diluvio Universale (Particolare)," "A Return to Earth"

Southwest Review: "The Body Translated into Heaven," "The Landscape of Memory"

The Yale Review: "Ovid at Land's End" (Probatio)

"A Brief History of Blasphemy for the Feast of the Assumption" appeared earlier in different form in *The 1002nd Night* by Debora Greger. Used by permission of Princeton University Press.

"Ovid at Land's End," Part Two, appeared as "Ovid on the Outer Cape" in *Off-Season at the Edge of the World* by Debora Greger. Reprinted by permission of the University of Illinois Press.

My deep thanks to Hazel O'Leary who, taking Bill Clinton at his word when he called for open government, opened the Hanford files.

Contents

Thus saith the Lord: What memories I have of thee, gracious memories of my youth, of the love that plighted troth between us, when I led thee through the desert, alone in the barren wastes, thou and I.

—JEREMIAH, 2.2

I will be a puff of wind in history, dust. Very few will remember me. Who remembers dust?

—FIDEL CASTRO

It was my job to say: "Radioactivity? What radioactivity? Oh, that radioactivity."

—TERRY PRATCHETT

The Landscape of Memory

I grew up in a desert. A desert twice over, second-growth desert—the first settlers, ranchers and orchardists, were forced out by the government in the 1940s to make way for the biggest stateside secret of the war, the building of the Hanford atomic plant. The plant, though even its workers hadn't known it at the time, made the plutonium for the bomb dropped on Nagasaki. The high school team was named the Bombers. The school ring had a mushroom cloud on it.

My father had a security clearance. I didn't know what he did for a living, just that he rode the bus out into the desert every day, like every other father I knew. At supper he'd tell us sometimes what he'd seen on the forty-mile trip—rabbits, deer, coyotes, goats gone wild. In winter the goats sheltered in a bank left standing where a town had been, the bank's cement walls too thick to be flattened. Perhaps he told us about this because he wasn't supposed to talk about work.

I grew up in the wind. Wind in the cottonwoods of the shelterbelt, then in the walls of the house, or filling your clothes, bringing you dust. Tumbleweeds rolled through town, down the streets named for dead army engineers, up the ones named for the trees from some greener world. Past the schools named for the white men who took that remote corner of the West from the Indians. Past the one

1

named for their Indian guide, and the one for a chief they defeated without killing. Past the neon atom spinning above the Uptown Theater, "uptown" a wild dream, a single block of shops two blocks north of "downtown" and its small handful of stores. Past the bowling alley, the Atomic Lanes.

This is the landscape by which all others are found wanting. The bare hills—such extravagance of browns and grays. The silvery browns. The brassy, coppery, golden grays. The Bois de Boulogne, the hills of Umbria, even Seattle just over the mountains—too green, too many trees. The canyons of Manhattan—so much to see, you couldn't see anything. Richland had more than enough sky. Wind was the landscape. It had swept out the past; the present was dust. I can almost taste it. The rain smelled sweetly of it. Even the snow was dusty. Even the dust, though we didn't know it then, was radioactive.

Adam's Daughter

Golden Transparent: by the light of an apple
I saw the earth, and it was green and good.
Under the dust it almost glowed. Gorged,
I lay in the back of the station wagon

between the boxes of apples my father had picked.
Golden Delicious: I had eaten of the fruit
of the knowledge of good and evil
but my eyes were not opened, I was no god.

No, I was a snake, well fed,
crushed beneath the heel of the desert air
heavy with isotopes. I was none the wiser.
Brought forth in sorrow, I was the daughter

of a radiation monitor, entry level,
who would work his way up to "feasibility studies"
for reactors yet to be built. Once a month
he left two glass flasks of his urine in a leaden case

on the front porch. Oh, let him not be "hot."
By the unearthly glow of an apple—
no, by the faint, sainted blue of atomic decay,
mother to daughter, uranium longed to be lead.

The cottonwoods of the shelterbelt shivered.
Leaves whispered rumors of nothing, nothing amiss.
A rattlesnake's lazy hiss turned on itself,
a cyclotron asleep in the dirt.

A train wailed like a prophet weary of wilderness.
In a lead-lined car, steel flasks of plutonium,
squeezed drop by drop from the rock,
tried not to be shaken by the world

outside the reactor gates. But what did I know?
As if out there at the checkpoint
a seraph had lifted a fiery sword.

The Desert Fathers

THE FLAGPOLE-SITTER

Forty days and forty nights:
down at the used car lot at the edge of town
a man had vowed to sit on top of a flagpole,
renouncing fleshly pleasures in the name of sales.

And from the radio stations there came men
in search of wisdom to pass on to their followers.
A hermit chained to his pillar in the desert,
the salesman broke his silence then—

but who remembers what he said?
He was as a field mouse clinging to a reed
shaken in the wind. He missed his Elvis.
The nuns said Elvis moved like sin. Like Khrushchev,

who pounded on the table with his shoe.
A man who sat in quiet, the old Desert Father said,
and heard the reeds in the wind
had not the same quiet in his heart.

Down to earth, the customers came by twos
to test the great finned arks lined up.
Noah the owner breathed on a rear-view mirror,
then rubbed out the desert with his sleeve.

And if a pillar of cloud rose out there,
invisible, from the reactor and drifted overhead,
it was top secret, or accident, or both—
we didn't need a seer to tell us that.

We wouldn't be told. Across the road
cow and steer would nuzzle the barbed wire,
chewing their contaminated cud,
eyeing the river swollen in spring flood.

The Age of Reason

O eternity, O Sunday afternoon:
just as the nuns had said, it stretched forth,
even more endless than I could imagine.

I was seven. The age of reason, Aquinas said,
who reasoned how many angels exactly
could crowd on the head of a pin. In a dress

unreasonably white I made my First Communion.
The host, tasting of neither body nor bread,
just library paste, stuck to the roof of the mouth.

"Old enough to know better," my father said,
but still, that eternal Sunday supper,
I played with my food. I even sat still,

watching the fat on the platter congeal, like a miracle.
The last of the Sunday beef tongue lolled,
silenced by the knife's sharp word.

Outside a leaf took its time to fall, bad angel,
down through the well-scrubbed floor of heaven,
down to the dirty, unreasonable desert.

Out there somewhere uranium broke down
into its no-more-stable daughters.
O half-life, O eternity:

sometimes we had to crouch under our desks at school
as if to pray even harder,
but we would be saved, if only from the Russians.

"And did you drink the milk as a child?"
the doctor will ask, the voice of reason.
"Milk from the dairy downwind?"

Andante pastorale

And then, to prove that I was wrong
to take the polonaise so fast,
Sister Immaculata raised her long skirts
just far enough to show how it was danced.

O those devout, black-stockinged ankles!
She curtsied to her missing partner
as if to the prince whose ring she wore, the Lord.
And rose reborn, and took a mincing step

in the most sensible of shoes,
and slowly twirled her heavy habit
into a gown of silk, her coif a powdered wig.
There in the convent basement,

I was her footman, who'd once been a rat.
And then, in that sparse cell of a practice room
beneath the fallout shelter sign,
I was back in school uniform,

just a rat who hadn't practiced.
School was out, the watery desert air
thickened with joyous, savage shouts.
Molecules swirling, wrapped in dust,

the air was thick with isotopes
that we knew nothing about.
The cries grew small, the perfect *decrescendo*
drawing out its dying

for the fathers who waited at the corner
for the swing-shift bus to the reactor.
Only I was left inside.
The radiator hissed in my direction.

The clock refused to tell the truth.
Behind closed doors, the convent cook
boiled vegetables until they confessed.
A cauliflower's brain was washed.

And Sister Immaculata righted the crucifix
she wore over her plain black heart,
and sat to play a little piece by Bach,
though he was a Protestant,

a Prussian, as good as an East German.
His "Air of Resignation" flooded that desert
of a room, as spare as the rain
that hovered angelically over us,

each note drying as it fell, never enough—
was that what resignation meant?
I asked my mother later, in despair
over both hands ever playing together.

" 'Sheep May Safely Graze,' " she read
over my shoulder, dishcloth in hand.
The notes were just a woolly blur.
She wiped a white key a little whiter.

I wiped my eyes again.
Sheep may safely, while their shepherd—
what of the goats my father told us about?
He saw them sometimes on his way to work,

the ones left behind, gone wild in the desert,
out where the bus went past the ghost ranches
of the nuclear reservation.
Awake, awake, ye sheep that wander.

The Blessing of the Throats

Two candles crossed, tied with a ribbon,
were held to each throat by the priest
who, in the way of adults when they came close,

seemed far away as he blessed each child,
praying the same few words over and over
in language so holy it was dead:

it was the feast of St. Blaise, caught in his cave
in the desert by hunters who saw him
lay his hands on their wounded prey,

then on the throat of a boy
whose mother would bring bread and candles
to the saint in prison—such was his torture,

his longing just to be made a martyr.
I longed for a sign, a mark on my skin
where the candles had cross-questioned my faith.

I longed to swallow the hint of a bruise,
to sing the silly hymn
from a throat as pure as the lily

that sang in silence above the quavering candles.
I longed to be nine
but only my eight-year-old voice came out,

as flat, as small as the earth,
a voice prophesying nothing,
crying in the desert.

       ■ ■

It was still February 3,
the year long lost. Snow hid the desert,
the tumbleweeds top secret,

sagebrush suddenly confidential.
Only our fathers were cleared.
They bundled control rods into the reactor.

We bundled into our boots and coats
to fight our own Cold War in the backyard.
I rubbed the face of my nearest enemy

in snow, and had my neck scrubbed raw.
Out in the desert a man would submit
to a full-body scrub, and pray

the Geiger counter would declare him saved.
Crystals irradiant, snow from a fist
tasted whiter than the host, melting faster,

burning the tongue that begged for mercy,
begging for more. Hungary had fallen.
Where we fell, we left snow angels sprawled.

A snowman stayed where it had fallen,
skin melting, the blinded eyes grown up,
two lumps of coal turned heavenward.

All-seeing, they saw nothing untoward.
The snowy altar cloth of the sky—
no, it was dark, much later,

nearly the year when a woman my age
would lift her hand to her throat,
and turn downwind,

as if you could see anything there,
where an odd cluster of cancers would be found.

Memories of the Atomic Age

O weigh
down these memories
with a stone
—OLIVE SENIOR

ROOT CELLAR

The night before, the garden had been caught
by frost. Now it lay blackened, slumped, a can
of rain's isotopes turned ice, a man's
work glove gone stiff, not even the fire hot.

The wet leaves slow to catch, he dug a well
in the not-yet-frozen dirt, more just a hole
with a door to keep out what would otherwise befall
the poor root vegetables. Now even hell

could freeze, my father said. A spark like a rocket
fell back to earth. Potatoes would grow eyes
to see in the dark, turnips turn coats like spies,
parsnips send out feelers in that dank pocket.

A shooting star—no, Sputnik raced the moon.
Time to wrestle with long division soon.

BLANK PAPER

He brought home paper from work, marked
   CONFIDENTIAL,
a briefcase full, now stamped DECLASSIFIED,
for us to draw on, mysteriously dull
but blank as snow on the other side.

Hoping we'd be quiet after work?
We played with the badge with his picture on it,
grew bored, and fought to be the dime-store clerk
you bought arms from, who wanted more than a chit.

Did my father dread the Saturdays it snowed?
Where was the hush of a world brought to a halt
at the reactor's gate, the badge you showed?
He made the sidewalk safe for us with salt.

My mother forced a paperwhite to bloom,
pure as the snow's irradiated room.

The altar blazed with flowers banked with lights
whose faith still flickered. Jesus wore a necklace.
The golden monstrance held the host in place
for forty hours. Like graveyard shift, those nights

in the desert guarding the reactor against sleep?
Your daughter prayed against Communists at school,
and now you both stood a moment in the vestibule.
Out in the desert ranged the ghostly sheep

whose shepherd had been bought by the government.
Bought, the rancher and the orchardist. O bless
the stubborn, contaminated fruit. And bless
the gases kept secret, released by accident,

the heavy water censing the river it warmed.
O bless and keep Your flock from any harm.

BURIAL MOUND

And that, my father said, was a burial mound.
And there we dug, and sifted the dusty dirt
all afternoon, a few trade beads a start:
such was our Sunday trespass on holy ground.

A deep blue bead from Venice, out in the desert—
where you can't go now unless it's just to golf.
Gone the Black Robes. Gone the dust-furred wolf.
What's to keep the reactor's guard alert?

The red of cheat grass a mirage that stained
the heat that wavered down the road that shone
like water made of dust so sweetly bitter—

flying home, you see the mounds from the plane.
Reactor cores, nuclear submarines,
buried out there for want of anything better.

Ship Burial

HANFORD, WASHINGTON

Take these treasures, earth, now that no one
Living can enjoy them.

—*BEOWULF*

On great stone wings a hawk hovered
in the great dusty hall of the sky.
Below, in the shade of a lowly sagebrush,
a rabbit dug its own grave.

An official sang out from time to time
sharply, almost dreamily,
to a bulldozer pushing back the earth,
back where it came from,

as if to plunge a great ship
deeper into the dirt.
That the dead might make the voyage
from this world to the next more easily,

the ship bore bread and candles,
irradiated fuel rods, the half-lives
of mother and daughter isotopes,
stout leather shoes.

Like gold leaf, the dust scattered.
Over the ship set adrift,
the wind hurried the waves of sand,
the hill dead ahead.

Coffee was poured from its flask,
the dregs flung upon the ground.
So in the desert they buried the heart
of the nuclear submarine.

Lives of the North American Martyrs

A clearing, Indian summer, 1646—
    to aid the digestion
Sister Superior read to us after lunch
    from the brief lives
of the North American martyrs.

    Of the heart cut out
of one before he died. Of Isaac Jogues,
    whose hand was mutilated
by the Iroquois. He lived on, marked
    for a Mohawk tomahawk.

I was nine or ten, practicing at lunch
    to hold a sandwich
with just the third and fourth fingers:
    thus St. Isaac held the host,
given dispensation by the Pope.

    Pouring the wine
he told the silence was the dead god's blood,
    and longed for martyrdom.
Even the dead silence was heathen.
    Each burning bush

an ambush, open-armed,
        each leaf the red
of vestments for a martyr's feast—
        Sister Superior
closed the book at the flaying.

■ ■

A clearing in the forest, Indian summer—
        no, on the playground
after recess was over, only a devil spun,
        the only dust
the nuns couldn't exorcise.

        The seven veils
of the wind danced before our gritty eyes.
        What would tempt us? Lunch?
Lunch was a head of cabbage on a platter.
        The desert lay in wait,

more infinite than God, no less remote.
        Somewhere out there
our fathers worked. They put on garments
        as white as the lily
to protect themselves from their work.

        They gloved their hands.
They laid their hands on the remote controls
        of robot hands.
A pair of steely pincers pinched the air
        behind the glass

as if to test its purity.
     Was it worthy
to hold a handful of uranium
     out of the reach
of gods, their dust and ash?

Northwest Passage

The portage, as I remember,
was long and not the last, and treacherous,
the Shoshone woman perhaps to be trusted
to guide them through hostile territory,

perhaps not. And when they came at length to nothing
but swamp, there was nothing to be done but wade in,
flintlock and powder held over their heads,
Lewis and Clark going first,

up to their armpits in the oozing Technicolor,
the drive-in movie burning like the visions
the nuns at school told us the saints saw,
burning in the desert.

And then I too slipped deeply
into sleep, a sated visionary,
because next we were driving home
past the mouth of the Yakima River,

the farthest up the Columbia Lewis and Clark went
before they turned back, making their way finally
to what they'd come for—open water.
Or so a sign we passed always claimed,

our one scrap of history.
I tasted the word like the host at Communion,
without the teeth, as the nuns had instructed,
until it dissolved into nothing.

Tonight someone else's father stood on the corner
in his shirtsleeves in the halo of streetlight,
waiting for the bus to take him deep in the desert:
it was time for graveyard shift at the reactor.

The moon was a canoe tipped over in the river,
the river heavy, warmed by coolant from the reactor.
Along the shore you found the pearly husks
of salmon, eyes wide, swimming with cloud.

Down to the Sea of the West, Lewis wrote,
along the banks, out over the water,
the tribes had built platforms to fish from,
so many they were almost continuous.

"And did you eat fish from the river
more than once a week when you were a child?"
the doctor will ask, but not for years yet,
not for years.

A Brief History of Blasphemy
for the Feast of the Assumption

HANFORD

What did you go into the wilderness to see?
A reed shaken with the wind?
Thorns have come up in the farmhouse abandoned,
nettles and brambles in the bulldozed barn.

Thirty miles into the well-guarded emptiness,
graveyard shift labors under the containment dome
of the reactor, honey to be drawn
from the rock, oil out of shale,

a rose to bloom in the desert,
its cloud of petals bursting forth,
triumphal, from a stalk of steam—
no, what did you go into the desert to see?

Your fathers about their business
in their white coveralls and safety shoes?
Uranium bombarded until it became dangerous,
the daughters you must be cleared to see,

there being nothing to see?
Radio-iodine rained on the derelict orchard.
A reed shaking in the wind,
what did you go into the wilderness to see?

NAGASAKI

An August morning, 1945,
the sky clearing but for a few airplanes,
wings glinting, unreadable
in the slanted Pacific sun,

the plum blossoms of parachutes
opening over a city just waking
that in the next choked breath
would rise in a pillar of smoke.

But not yet. Please, not yet
the plane turning steeply away
into history empty,
full throttle into the sun.

Let a missionary still rehearse
some Christian hymns in the ash,
the fleet's dirge yet to be sung
over the burned water

by the choir of the burned.
Let the fire and local brimstone rain down
lesser plagues in blessing
on those cursed to survive.

The church was too warm. Sickly, too sweet,
flowers forced into bloom in the desert
that was the fifties were sacrificed
on the side altar at the Virgin's woody feet.

The air conditioners feebly roared.
The organ tried its lungs and groaned,
drowning the drone of the priest.
Someone's mother fainted at his polished feet.

Someone's father left Mass early
for the first shift at the reactor.
Who needed intercession by the mother of God?
The angel Plutonium would keep us safe.

And so we celebrated the new holy day of obligation,
the Virgin's assumption into heaven
no longer just *probable opinion*,
denial of which would be blasphemous,

but declassified at last,
her body no longer top secret,
long missing from some unremarked tomb,
but explained away by the doctors of the church

who wound an empty shroud around their cleverness:
her body was conveyed on a cloud to heaven,
it was official,
just as the heretic had written long ago.

The Cloud of Unknowing

*It is the shortest work of all that a man can imagine. It is
neither longer nor shorter than an atom which is defined
. . . as the smallest division of time, and it is so short . . .
it is indivisible and almost incomprehensible. This is the
time of which it is written: "You will be asked how you
spent all the time that has been given to you."*

— *THE CLOUD OF UNKNOWING*

Why did I not die at birth,
for then I should have lain down
and been quiet?

I should have lain in the dirt
beside those who fought over it,
under the ruins built in their name,

while they lamented
the cities they destroyed and rebuilt,
ash after ash, dust laid to dust.

I should have lain in the dirt,
looking up like the man
who put a dark cloud between himself and his god,

the better to see him.
I should have been the woman looking up:
the waters of the sky parting,

only a few parachutes drifting low,
        testing the wind.
And then the darkness covered the earth.

        That was the second cloud.
She wiped her hands clean.
        Her skin came off in her hands.

Why did I not lie down in the river
        with the rest of them?
Invisible in the cloak of flesh,

        I should have been dust
lamenting the dust whose daughter I am.
        O dust wrapped in wind,

in the desert I found these words
        where they had burned
and put the ash on my tongue.

I mentioned guilt in a talk I once gave in Rome, and it was translated over the earphones as gold leaf. South of the Alps guilt has only its legal or criminal sense. The rest is all bella figura.

— W. H. AUDEN

Psyche and Eros in Florida

In the subtropics it must be spring:
a flock of cedar waxwings
swarms the cabbage palm.
It clings to its shadow. They whisper.

They devour the fruit no local bird wants.
Unswerving, they swerve through clotheslines.
Let their whispery cries be mine.
Their whisper of wings is yours.

But what good is sight?
In the dark, I thought, lay the struggle
of mind over body that kept Aquinas awake.
Whoever you were, you slept on.

By candlelight nothing is not beautiful.
The relief of your finely sculpted head.
The drop of wax that fell on your bare shoulder.
Why didn't you want me to see you?

The drop of red on each wing almost glows
this hour neither dark nor light.
Waxwings, forgive me. Fly away north.
What was the dark like?

I remember the mind fogged with something not dream.
And afterwards
what of the traitorous, languorous body?
It lies down. It begs.

Nights of 1995

in memory of James Merrill

> *Even the fowles*
> *Were sad for Orphye, and the beast with sorye syghing howles:*
> *The rugged stones did moorne for him, the woods which many a tyme*
> *Had followed him to heere him sing, bewayled this same cryme.*
> *Yea even the trees lamenting him did cast theyr leavy heare.*
> *The rivers also with theyr tears (men say) encreased were.*
>
> —OVID

Profligate with loss,
the live oak wept the old leaves down;
one pine needle stitched the air
a shroud to enfold one last song.

Come back once more.
Come as far as the wild plum.
It blooms like snow
and then its white-hot grief is gone.

Just to the edge of the yard,
the edge left raw of the upper world.
Stay here in the plum's white shade.
Trees of the underworld refuse to unburden;

come back to the Coffee Cafe in Milledgeville
so "cleverly named," your letter said last fall.
Let the name stop you again,
you whose words come back to haunt us.

Come after hours, even.
You'll be the ashen one in the corner
whose hand is raised, the bones still beautiful.
Seeing through you, who don't want anything,

the waitress will go home. The last clean cup
still overturned, a planchette-in-waiting—
where did you leave your Ouija board?
Oh, rattle the cup until it gives up one last word.

Call us. Call us out of the animal.
The dead are good tonight but I,
just the raccoon rustling the trash out back,
will lift my quivering snout

from the delicate ribs of a chicken.
Crouch down. Tomorrow I'll remember nothing
though a rank scent persists on my paws.
Put on your mask, your domino. I lift my voice

like a scrap of meat, into a monody.
This hill of beans. That girl I once was,
asleep somewhere, still at her books.
A language dead, the casket rusted shut.

Ave atque vale.

Ovid at Land's End

The camels wake up complaining
just like the rest of us.
Sunday afternoon at the Holiday Inn
they show *Lawrence of Arabia*

in the dining room for anyone bored
by the shrieking gulls, the drowning buoys.
A man lies down in the sand to wait—
how better to work up a thirst?

Happy the happy, for they shall have Happy Hour.
The boy in the front row plays
at driving the camels again.
The rest of us nurse our drinks.

You can almost taste the dirt,
and I've had worse. Here at the oasis
there's no movie that can't be drawn out
reel by interrupted reel:

four hours stretch to five, to six
as a blond, blue-eyed speck makes its way
dune by dune across the wall.
What does he want—to bury himself in the dust?

But only back in the Empire's uniform
does he go unrecognized.
The bird bathing in the dirt by the roadside
may be your worst comrade, a gracious enemy,

but I remain as always yours,
though these years I have had no word.
Next month perhaps a coast trader
will brave the last ice in the harbor

and add this letter to his stale cargo.
Oh, for a sailor with whom to speak
some rusty, half-forgotten words!

EPILOGUS

I paint my shaven face
the way I remember my wife made up hers
for our last night on the town,
the capital of memory, the exile's eternal city.

There are nights here, such nights,
but not much town. What there is
is narrow, a few fishermen, a few fur coats
in winter's unemployment line,

which snakes weekly through the choir loft
of the church turned makeshift public library,
the old one burned by the volunteer fireman
who always got to fires first.

Merciful the mirror that's fogged—
you wouldn't recognize this wreck
who creaks and groans, here run aground.
The foghorn bemoans its lot.

The red seaweed has been dried and crushed;
on the cheekbone is rubbed the blush of innocence,
the lips reddened to a knowing gash.
To the eyelid, lashes of mink

glued clump by clump. My wig is frosted,
my breasts of foam uplifted.
I have poured myself into a sheath
as if, though parted,

she and I could be one body.
In her shell I teeter crabwise,
the hermit Hermaphroditus in heels,
queen of the beach,

past the *O Vacancy* sign
burning this weekend in honor
of the transvestites' convention.
The tourists gone home for the season

have nothing on us,
who live at one of the ends of the earth,
at the shore of the Underworld.
Who use their coins

to close the eyes of our dead,
that the dead, dressed in their finest,
faces painted back to health,
have something to pay the ferryman.

The foghorn mourns longest,
not knowing what it mourns.
The stones my neighbors,
who will not have me,

lie drying into dullness
even under cloud. I send you one—
does the faintest of heartbeats ripple
under the smooth, the ageless skin?

No, the former Luftwaffe pilot
now enjoys life as a woman.
Emperor, I pray that you may always
disbelieve what I have said.

Bureau de change

Was it Ovid who counted out the lire?
I weighed the strange handful of change
in a Rome where weeds ruled the ruins
briefly, a brutal flowering. Quick,

open the guidebook to press a bloody poppy!
Shoes full of dust, ruined,
we climbed the stairs to the Hotel Termini,
next to the Hotel Everest.

A dragging numbness by the fifth story,
the limbs becoming wood—
was this the deep languor Daphne felt at last,
pursued out of love by a god

until she begged her father the river
to make her less beautiful?
Two sagging beds could narrowly be made one
in the shady room where the dry bark

of my hand touched his sun-warmed skin.
He removed a leaf from my hair,
one hand around my ankle—
I recognized this from dream,

the swimming up through leaves toward light
from the earth you couldn't quite leave alone.
What would Freud say, Publius Ovidius?
Some ordinary misfortune

was all you had a girl long for.
The gods turned her into a boy.
You must change your life?
You must change your money first.

Sunday at the Ruins

Go thou to Rome,—at once the Paradise,
The grave, the city and the wilderness.

—SHELLEY

How young they look, the bride and groom,
like the saints in old paintings,
luminous, too hot in their finery.

Not quite themselves nor quite
each other's yet, they stiffen,
posed as if by a long-ago painter

against the only landscape he ever used,
no matter whose story was to be illuminated.
The love of ruin, the ruin of love—

she teeters against her husband of an hour,
wanting her picture taken
by the little Temple of Vesta,

though the attribution's uncertain.
The groom wants her by the Temple
of Manly Virtue instead,

though it's named without foundation,
its scabrous columns peeling.
Love, how young they look,

the bride brushing her long archaic skirt,
brushing off the long history of dirt.
Was it like that with us?

A couple of tourists dismayed
to find nothing, not even churches, open,
have we strayed from our lives

into the shot? Was it ever like that?
Oh, tie the knotgrass tighter.
Sweeten the berries of the wild bittersweet.

In the Eternal City

By the Baths of Caracalla I sat down and wept,
licking the dust from my lips, reptilian,
as glutted with ruin as an emperor,
and these my subjects:
the upstart weeds I trampled in the dirt.

I wanted a bath, even if it were dust.
A strigil to scrape the skin
that I couldn't crawl out of.
I wanted to be rubbed raw,
the towel roughened with perfume,

and then to lie, cold-blooded,
skin to skin on a smooth broken column.
I wanted—but it didn't matter
in the city of the dead.
The loosestrife shuddered where the nettle crept.

Shelley was right: the dead survive us.
Over the place they made bloody
and the one their slaves made clean,
I passed as a pilgrim
looking for a place to have lunch.

As tenderly as an emperor
who found his appetite refined
by a morning at the Colosseum
that saw, more rare than a Christian,
a hippotigris slain,

the lizard that had crawled out beside me
waited in the dust to be served.
Not even its eye moved, stone set in stone,
as if this afternoon were the afterlife.
As for the enemy, Caracalla made his peace.

As for his own people, he had some dismissed,
others killed. "Cease praying,"
he wrote to the Senate,
"that I may be emperor for a hundred years."
And then the lizard's tongue lashed the back of the air.

         ▪ ▪

O Shelley, even in death you would come here,
though the labyrinth of weeds you loved is gone.
Gone the green waste wilderness,
the snowlike columns melted away.
Sea-monstrous, you drift, shadow to shadow,

still clutching your Winckelmann,
a finger marking your place.
Your face and arm are gone, your ashes cold
A scent grows sickly, so thickened with perfume,
the arches dizzy, the stairs ruined.

Your nankeen trousers have been washed,
your white silk stockings mended.
The copy of Sophocles that they found,
torn where you gripped it,
has long since dried in the sun.

Were the sea to overflow the earth,
you wished of such ruin,
but only a leaf gone to gold,
curled on its keel, sails the dust,
hugging the ruined shore.

The Love of Ruins

Happy, alas, too happy
—DIDO, *THE AENEID*

Happy the weeds that invaded the ruins,
happier the children who trample them.
Where is the silence we were promised,
old wind happy just to stir old dust?

The flames of poppies Dido might have loved
as much as her washed-up Trojan,
whatever they augured—how happily they smolder,
embers aglow in the fresh air.

Would you have left her for this?
Even the snack bar is closed for restoration.
A sparrow pecks over the crumbs
from tourist sack lunches, late tribute

to the home lives, never dull, of gods.
Just ahead, a couple come from another country
to argue in the dust about the dust.
The past is nothing without us.

Four teenage girls have peeled off their sweaters
and lain to sun, fallen caryatids
not old enough not to be beautifully bored.
From all that remains of the Temple of Love,

the great steps we've climbed to nothing,
we overlook the swath of motorway,
a few sheep left to guard the Tiber
where it once bent. Where at last

Aeneas made landfall, the guidebook Virgil claims.
To keep his little empire from crumbling
before the train back to the present arrives,
a schoolteacher has divided his class

against itself for a game of feints and parries.
Boys against girls, girls against dust,
they scream with happiness they can't contain.

Keats in Ohio

How long is this posthumous life of mine to last?
—KEATS TO HIS DOCTOR

A clearing somewhere
in the lost forests of Ohio,
        the last leaves
a brilliant library of loss.
        A river of mist.
A sawmill's smoke and feathers

        hung in the still gold air,
each ghost tree planed straight and true.
        In the river
the muskrat burrows deeper.
        On the bank
a shirt so clean it glows,

        bride white,
against the fires of fall—
        how nuptial
the world trimmed in white
        on its way to death,
blade and leaf enlaced in frost.

This is the coldness
needed to make the sweetness sweet,
        the sugar maples know,
the leaves inflamed, the air too red
        to breathe, as if,
parting the branches, into the clearing

        a man would step who,
from a hired carriage reeling toward Rome,
        had seen two footmen
in the Campagna assist a cardinal.
        One loaded the gun for him,
one like a good dog beat the bushes

        to flush the songbirds
favored in the Eternal City.
        In a rented room
Death would keep watch over his sleep
        as it worsened,
over the friend who sketched him sleeping

        to keep himself awake,
over the hired English nurse.
        Death held the bridle
of the hired horse, held out of reach
        the bottle of laudanum
Severn had been sent to buy,

the ship awaiting
a breath of wind back at Gravesend.
Still the slow rush
of water toward water, the boat
of a fountain
drowning in sorrow the piazza below.

Still the rushed slow fall
of leaves. They bury the Spanish Steps,
small belongings
to be swept up and burned,
the air crisp with regret—
what was left for him to despair?

The Flea Market at the End of History

And then at dawn you take the bus
across the river to the end of the world,
where on the seventh day no one rests,
where history ends, broken up to be sold.

Past the vast chipped bowl of the Colosseum,
rosy, not bloody, in the first escalade of light,
past the lathered horses of mist
that lap seven times the vanished Circus Maximus

to entertain the bored ghost of an emperor,
the bus bears its load of locals who take no notice.
Across the Tiber where the world once ended
in the long-lanced grass of Etruscan sheep meadow,

Sunday the tongues of church bells loosen,
wagging the fleas of the faithful to market.
To seven times seven secondhand hills—
far off, a hill of blue jeans fading toward snow.

Closer, a well-worn hill of shoes. The smallest,
a handful of coins dug from a realm so long ago
they're worthless and too dear to touch.
Whose acid likeness wore them down to this?

The augur disemboweling a chicken
has foretold a revolution in the skillet.
On a hot-plate altar, an offering burnt
for the crowd assembled at his feet.

Where's the old circus performer who liked the most
to be wrapped in chains, the chains then locked
to make his smooth, but not too smooth, escape
the more miraculous? The pickpocket misses him.

At the perimeter, from open suitcases,
Russians offer whatever they could carry out.
Icons look ready to weep in the day's hard light.
Where are the shoppers whose prayers they could
    answer?

Stout wooden dolls hide one inside the other
from the high-powered East German binoculars
one suitcase over. Long gone, the local concrete
passed off as Berlin Wall.

A Pole who looks like my father—wheaten hair,
the wide face Stoic without meaning to be,
the landlocked, watery blue eyes—
has laid out crisp, unused zlotys, the day's best,

the most pure, most worthless bargain.

Much Too Late

"Much too late," I said on the steps
of Santa Maria Maggiore, meaning it wasn't a ruin,
we could find something older and take each other's
    picture.

But you insisted and then we were inside,
the dim tonnage polished to a hush,
the guidebook proving you right:

not the apse built with the rubble of pagan Rome,
not the sliver of the Holy Infant's crib in silver,
the porphyry urn of early martyr's bones,

but the ceiling. It rated a star in your book.
There was the first gold Columbus brought back
with the first slaves from the New World

to prove he was as good as his word.
The Queen gave it to the Pope to prove she was good.
On high, the papal coat of arms bristled with gilt,

the keys to the kingdom of heaven forever crossed,
flanked by plastered, impossible flowers.
High on the wall a mosaic flickered like faith:

a dreamer who'd hung around the courts
of the great all his life, which is to say
Moses, the man in the plainest robe,

still stretched out his rocky hand
to part a rocky patch of sea,
sure he'd been chosen by God,

sure the promised land showed up in a later panel—
though it never did, only the scouts sent ahead
to search for it, lost in the surrounding gold.

Thirty days and thirty nights in the desert
that was the ocean—too late for Columbus
to order the ships to turn back,

too late for him not to believe he was sent.
The ships hung in the eye of the wind,
the scent of dirt carried over the salt.

Much too late, we two Americans,
and this the wrong god to ask forgiveness of.

I have seen a vast number of paintings, palaces, and churches and received far more "impressions" than I know what to do with. One needs a companion to help him dispose of this troublesome baggage.

—HENRY JAMES IN VENICE

He had ordered dinner from some Tratteria, and while waiting its arrival . . . we stood out on the balcony, in order that, before the daylight was quite gone, I might have some glimpses of the scene the Canal presented. Happening to remark, in looking up at the clouds, which were still bright in the west, that "what had struck me in Italian sunsets was that peculiar rosy hue——" I had hardly pronounced the word "rosy" when Lord Byron, clapping his hand on my mouth, said, with a laugh, "Come, damn it, Tom, don't be poetical."

—THOMAS MOORE IN VENICE

Light is half a companion.

—GENOESE PROVERB

The Patron Saint of Venice

Oh, tourist,

is this how this country is going to answer you . . . ?

—ELIZABETH BISHOP

There, barely out of the water, lay the harbor,
low, the sea deep green, the only scenery
except the faded blue of far-off mountains.
Only on window ledges was there greenery.

There was the island of glassblowers, bricked over.
A sunken island, one the tide had glazed blue.
Isle of the dead. Isle of the tourists,
famed for its mirrors. All you saw was you,

an island adrift in a sea of guided tours.
There was the island dwarfed by a freighter,
an island of pastry flaking on a green glass shelf.
Tour guides were drowned by church bells, eight or

nine waves rolling the piazza under, unsettling
the dust, sinking the last, the fondest hope
of the tourist at the tobacconist's
to be pilgrim in search of more than stamps and soap.

To be gondolier singing tourists to supper, his foot
pushing a wall away from his boat as his voice swelled,
just a Venetian singing a Neapolitan song,
ducking the footbridge lest the high note fall.

To be the man selling ices to tired tourists.
He wanted to go to Florida. The rag
he wiped his hands on had gone gray with sweetness.
Disney World, *Miami Vice*—their flags

unfurled over gelati the color of marble,
the meaty stones before which Ruskin swooned.
Was this travertine James's favorite?
Or that Turner sky dug up with a spoon?

Oh, to be the mosaicist brought from Byzantium,
the one that later centuries would find inferior,
who worked the glitter around another saint
whose name means nothing now. The interior

of the basilica dirty, aglow—
who remembered where each pillar was plundered?
No angle true but every one devout.
Oh, to be just the shellfish the tide held under.

I Dinosauri di Venezia

The past is empty:
the bones have been dug up
    out of love,
numbered, bathed in shellac
    and swathed in plaster
for the long journey to the *Museo*
    di storia naturale,
where Tyrannosaurus is still rex,
    the dainty forelegs
still too short to reach the terrible mouth.
    Where a nest of eggs,
potato-size, is too petrified to hatch.
    A duckbilled herbivore
come late, forehead as bent as a doge's hat,
    brain walnut-size,
skin rendered the same unlikely green
    as the Grand Canal—
shall a last doge be married to the lagoon?
    Patch the old wedding barque!
O Love, where's the gold ring
    to be thrown overboard,
quick, before the going gets rough?

    The past is crushing:
in this sinking palazzo here's a footprint
    to prove it, left
by a creature weightier and more ancient

than the parent my age
who's holding forth deep in Triassic ooze
one floor down.
Swarmed by children who are in heaven—
whatever it is in Italian—
in the Cretaceous, the past is desert,
a three-toed gully
filled with later, paler sand:

Days crossing the badlands
delivered us at last not to the farm
where fossils were
the unwanted, ever-bearing crop
but to this:
roadside dinosaurs rearing their tiny, lofty heads
to look down at us.
Were we, not they, late for lunch?
I was just six,
riding nowhere on the back of a Triceratops.

How small my parents looked,
lost against the leggy pillars of a Brontosaurus,
hardly parents anymore,
hardly mine. How coolly the concrete
of the huge bodies
suffered my slight, warm-blooded touch.
O extinct age! O Rapid City!

The Body Translated into Heaven

One bell and then another,
more separate for ringing so close together,
breaking the emptiness missing before
into the fullness missing after:

so, out of love, one body leaves another
to draw on clothes,
turning toward the window,
toward the city built on water,

the water crushed by the weight
of the light until it's broken glass,
the salt-thickened light dissolved
into tears lost in translation.

So, in the mosaic of the *translatio*
where thieves steal the body of a saint,
hiding it in a cask of salt pork
so the stench of sanctity won't alert the guards,

a ship waits to translate the relics
across a sea treacherously empty, only gold.
So, in the twilight perpetual in the basilica,
the saint enters his body again

to guide the ship past the shipwreck faithfully waiting.
So the lamps before the high altar waver,
wanting the dim light off the body as much
as the slit of sun from outside piercing its stone.

So, in the eternally lit shrine
of a side-street shop window,
mannequins hold their long pose longer
for adoration after hours.

Eyes only for us, like those of saints
otherwise engaged, their long Byzantine limbs
modestly covered stitch by stitch
in skintight designer knits,

these punk martyrs in jewel-studded raptures,
unmoved, tempt the pious pocketbook
to translate the body into a vision by Versace.
O, the price tag in lire pronounces,

OOO, prayer just holy breathing,
O, as the mystic long proclaimed.
So how does that translate into dollars?
So Polo saw the mouths of the dead stuffed with pearls.

The Further Travels of Marco Polo

You who would travel in my footsteps,
who come as far as the church no longer a church,
the stone with my name on it no longer there,
who stop at the door in the dirt,

come a little farther, carrying nothing.
Neither letters from the Pope, nor gifts,
not even a relic of the Holy Sepulcher,
not even water, nothing I carried

into the desert of deserts is of use now.
On the fourth day you come to a river
of fresh water digging its way underground,
and in its bed lie those stones called precious.

Thinking yourself still thirsty,
knowing yourself still merchant above ground,
you who are weary may stop to weigh yourself down.
If you remain behind, overtaken by sleep

such as you've never known—*so very full of dreams,*
that desert—you hear yourself called by name
in a tone you remember. From a door in the dark
a voice offers to buy the clothes off your body.

You look down—how did you come to be wearing your
    best?
Thus the dead amuse themselves. Likewise by day
they assume the appearance of traveling companions
who endeavor to conduct you out of your way,

as I have done, past the meal the living set for you
so lovingly they'll consume it themselves
after you've been offered just the fumes,
your mouth stuffed with pearls.

They wouldn't recognize you, gone so long
they think you're dead. I know. You're free
to marry here, where the wedding is drawn on paper,
bride and attendants in all their finery

shown with horses and other animals,
money, and every article of furniture,
and these, together with the marriage contract,
committed to flames that convey none of this

to the other world. But come a few days farther,
a few years on, where the water is greener
than the grass holding the dirt close overhead.
Water as green as the canals of home

and as bitter. You want to turn back?
You want, like the great Khan,
to refuse Death an audience?
Death is the lark's tongue you feed

to a prized falcon, Death.
Sew enough jewels into the lining of your coat
and the arrows glance off all the way home,
but it's not enough. Take this

and, like a great khan, have it read to you.
I, Marco, whose name is dirt now,
have not told half of what I saw.

In the Museum
of the Eighteenth Century

we were a few centuries late.
The guards had seen it all—
how the paintings looked down on the statues
and the tattered, roped-off chairs,
down on our jeans and sunglasses,
the cameras we were forbidden to use.

Angels came and went overhead,
bare under their banners.
A warrior so far out of uniform
that a flag fluttered where a fig leaf might go
could only look on. Porcelain vessels,
milky and plump, had been set out

to catch the late dust. Deep in the mirror
it was so dark no one looked back.
Whose footsteps echoed—how far off?
The little guard from two rooms ago
wanted us back and *hurry*, he mimed,
not needing our language to urge us along.

Where were the other guards?
He wanted us to take pictures,
though it was forbidden,
to love the room he loved most,
the little one where clowns,
fallen like angels, always wore white,

a hump where the wings would be.
And always a beaked, dark leather mask,
whether *The Clown in Love*,
his arm flung around a masked lady,
a hand on her breast, or *The Clown at Rest*,
fallen down drunk, there being no happiness

that couldn't be drowned or slept off.
Even in *The House of Clowns*
gravity got the best of a cartwheel.
There was a ladder—I knelt on the floor
to catch the great hole painted on the ceiling,
a last clown climbing out of this world.

No, one had fallen to earth in a dark suit—
on tiptoe the guard stood to kiss my cheeks,
kisses so swiftly sacramental they felt dirty.
The sputter of motorboat, the cry of gondolier—
somewhere outside, Venice sank a little deeper
into the present. Kiss me.

Kiss me like that before we go.

Il Diluvio universale (particolare)

Because whatever must happen
will happen by water,
Noah has sent a raven to look
for something not made of water.

Because in the story
told in mosaic stone by stone,
the bird has been distracted,
in the way of all omnivores,

by something that might be edible
floating in the floodwaters,
Noah must send out a dove.
It will be evening

by the time it returns
with a few leaves in its beak
and even that won't be sign enough.
He must wait for a bird

that doesn't come back,
wait at the window of the ark,
the shutters flung open
catching the first light

after long rain,
half silver, half gold,
at the edge of a room so dark
nothing can be seen

of the life he's built on water.
The white pelicans led aboard
several scenes back,
and the great gray herons—

are they still happy?
Who was assigned the lower decks?
And what of the sons who looked on,
clutched by their stiff, mystified wives,

as their father persuaded a pair
of eagles through a window?
Noah's face has a greenish cast,
whether seasickness or something holier,

it isn't clear, here in the basilica
where it is always evening,
whatever the story
that's been surrounded by gold left empty—

Noah later, the beached whale
of his body so old, so thickened,
so lovingly wasted by the mosaicist
stone by pale stone

that his smooth sons must look away
as they go on preparing forever
to cover his nakedness,
the skin already tinged

with the shades of the dead—
the tincture of ivory,
the several greenish grays,
the olive that turns a dark liver color—

though he's only drunk.
Whatever happens next
will not happen by water,
so God, so far above all this

only His hand appears, has promised.
So there will only be rain
of brimstone and fire,
which the master, rowed from Ravenna

to Venice to turn rain to stone,
has left for us to envision
in the dark ages
that no merely votive light can dispel.

A Return to Earth

It was the hour when Venice lay
not in darkness so much as underwater—
how else to explain the aquamarine depths
of five A.M., the city submerged
below the waterline of sleep?

Only a cat as sleek, as fast
as a fish passing through a water column,
prowled the piazza, too early for the pigeons
that would school in the shoals of tourists
having their picture taken, two by two.

The grand piano moored outside Florian's
was battened down for the night—
too late for a last sodden waltz.
Too early for a last sorrow to be drowned
at Harry's Bar, drowned itself in the dark.

Down the deep streets, over shallow canals
we drifted as in a dream toward open water,
floating at last up the water steps—
no, *down* to the waiting water taxi.
Two of every kind herded aboard:

two who'd been to Egypt and beyond
with matching suitcases the size of tombs.
Two Japanese women who slipped off their shoes
as if the boat were home. Two striped businessmen
scouting for dry land for sale.

And the two of us, mismatched
or grown alike out of love, who'd drifted for days
past the long, unfathomable marriage
of a city afloat on a promise of nothing
from an unforgiving sea.

■ ■

From the boat the city pulled away until it was
just a painting belonging to someone else,
then a postcard of a painting,
something you could hold later,
a drop of crimson lake still burning

to make true the water's untrue blues.
Back through the Byzantine mosaic of islands
held together by the water holding them apart,
the pilot steered. Past a stand
of black cypress in the rich black muck

low tide laid bare, the silence blackened.
Past the ghosts of the first marsh-dwellers.
Past their first harvest, salt.
Gone the watered silks, the silken masks,
the affairs conducted, masked, by water.

The city sank a little farther
into the water that wanted it back.
Terraferma was a dock at the end of a runway,
this the leaving called in those parts
"returning to earth." The last palazzi

of Istrian marble, the clouds—
the plane rose through them: nothing
but the fluff Tiepolo loved as much
as his large lush women, named for virtues—
the ones about to tumble

in all gravity not out of the sky
so much as out of their gowns,
too busy being virtuous to look down
from the ceiling of a grand ballroom
that overlooked the Grand Canal, no longer grand.

I remember the room flooded
with dirty light washed up from below.
The clouds at the back of the fresco,
gauzy, chalky, were another story:
the beaten exaltation of partial clearing

after long rain, a room no longer drifting
but run aground, held down by wind
that chilled what it enfolded,
so much to be thankful for
that you called it home.

The Desert Father

My father's about to step from the bus
after a long day out in the desert
of "the areas," each with its reactor.
In his large dry hands he'll be holding—

the way old saints were painted
holding tiny churches on great books—
a black lunch-box shaped like a barn,
a sheaf of declassified papers:

next to a sparrow bathing in dust,
just a man waiting in the desert
for a sudden whirlwind, *subitus turbo*,
to descend upon him—

                    at last I'd come
out of the wilderness that was Venice,
generation sinking unto generation,
to open water, the view as sudden as a vision.

Everything, even the sodden lagoon,
tilted toward me, gritty with light,
a great bowl of it breaking at my feet.
I was parched, ready for a drink:

Venice is desert, the old painters knew,
this the leafless light bathing the face
of each hermit painted waiting
for a sandy, favorable tide, a light

so blinding that a desert father squinting,
preoccupied, was all that was missing.
"The loneliness of the desert is Paradise,"
claimed St. Jerome.

Mass in B Minor

for George and Zara Steiner

Lord, have mercy on Bach the accused,
found guilty of tampering with the hymns.
Guilty also of smuggling a subversive,
a *girl*, into the choir loft to sing.

Have mercy on Bach,
whose choir practice ended in despair,
which is to say, in fisticuffs,
the Bach who brawled in the street for his art.

He wrote for money, who wrote for You.
Have mercy. Good Teuton,
he wrote a groveling letter to the Elector
and enclosed the Kyrie and Gloria.

Johann Sebastian: on the concert program
the high fence of his name had been erected,
guard towers charred in the same black-letter
as the book my father brought back from the war.

He pronounced its title for us: *Mein Kampf.*
And slid the enemy sword with just the scrape
of a grace note back into its scabbard.
A flag too heavy to unfold—

when had the swastika been removed?
The penciled names of the fallen
lay in the mass grave of a small notebook.
Christ, have mercy.

Have mercy on Bach, whose Sanctus saved no one,
not even the damned. Crystalline, cyclonic,
the Kyrie seeped through the chapel,
becoming what we breathed,

the prayer entering the body first.
The man next to me was just back from Poland.
"Let us arrange your taxi to Auschwitz,"
the sign in his hotel had read,

the flesh made word to dwell among us.

About the Author

Debora Greger is the author of four previous books of poems, *Movable Islands, And, The 1002nd Night,* and *Off-Season at the Edge of the World.* She has won, among other honors, the Grolier Prize, the Discovery/*The Nation* Award, the Peter I. B. Lavan Younger Poets Award, an Award in Literature from the American Academy and Institute of Arts and Letters, and the Brandeis University Award in Poetry. She has received the Amy Lowell Poetry Traveling Scholarship, and grants from the Ingram Merrill Foundation, the Guggenheim Foundation, and the National Endowment for the Arts. She teaches at the University of Florida and lives in Florida and in Cambridge, England.